Presented To

Presented By

Date

Peace I leave with you;

my peace I give you.

I do not give to you

as the world gives.

Do not let your hearts

be troubled

and do not be afraid.

—John 14:27 NIV

BLESSINGS

—*for the*—

EVENING

Finding Peace in God's Presence

SUSIE LARSON

BETHANY HOUSE PUBLISHERS
a division of Baker Publishing Group
Minneapolis, Minnesota

Published by Bethany House Publishers
11400 Hampshire Avenue South
Bloomington, Minnesota 55438
www.bethanyhouse.com

Bethany House Publishers is a division of
Baker Publishing Group, Grand Rapids, Michigan

Printed in China

Library of Congress Cataloging-in-Publication Data is on file at the Library of Congress, Washington, DC.

ISBN 978-0-7642-1163-8

Unless otherwise indicated, Scripture quotations are from the *Holy Bible*, New Living Translation, copyright © 1996, 2004, 2007 by Tyndale House Foundation. Used by permission of Tyndale House Publishers, Inc., Carol Stream, Illinois 60188. All rights reserved.

Scripture quotations identified HCSB are from the Holman Christian Standard Bible, copyright 1999, 2000, 2002, 2003 by Holman Bible Publishers. Used by permission.

Scripture quotations identified THE MESSAGE are from *The Message* by Eugene H. Peterson, copyright © 1993, 1994, 1995, 2000, 2001, 2002. Used by permission of NavPress Publishing Group. All rights reserved.

Scripture quotations identified NIV are from the Holy Bible, New International Version®. NIV®. Copyright © 1973, 1978, 1984, 2011 by Biblica, Inc.™ Used by permission of Zondervan. All rights reserved worldwide. www.zondervan.com

Scripture quotations identified NKJV are from the New King James Version. Copyright © 1982 by Thomas Nelson, Inc. Used by permission. All rights reserved.

Cover design by Brand Navigation

Interior design and art direction by Paul Higdon

Author is represented by The Steve Laube Agency

To my mom, Pat Erickson,
and Kev's dad, Dean Larson,
who lost their beloved spouses this year

May the promised blessing of seeing your
loved ones again bring comfort and
encouragement to your souls.
Love you so much.

To Jesus
May You breathe fresh life into every soul
who picks up this book.
Knowing that we get to spend eternity with
You is the greatest blessing of all.
You're our greatest treasure.

Contents

To You, My Friend

God loves you with an everlasting love. He is faithful, wise, and true. He is a miracle-working, soul-saving, life-transforming God. And He cares deeply about you.

As you work your way through these pages, may you grow to know—on a much deeper level—what you possess when you have Christ. He is above all, in all, and through all. He is the way, the truth, and the life. He promises never to leave you, never to forsake you, and never to let go of your hand. Life on earth is hard sometimes, but life with God is always good, always beautiful, and forever eternal. The Lord wants you to last long and finish strong, and He's the one who will keep you strong to the end.

May these blessings be yours in every way.

—*Susie Larson*

One more thing: Don't miss the blessings near the end of the book for specific needs and occasions, including Sabbath Rest, Grief, Thanksgiving Day, Christmas, Spiritual Warfare, and Disappointment.

Blessings for the Evening

separate us from God's love. Neither death nor life, neither angels nor demons, neither our fears for today nor our worries about tomorrow—not even the powers of hell can separate us from God's love. No power in the sky above or in the earth below—indeed, nothing in all creation will ever be able to separate us from the love of God that is revealed in Christ Jesus our Lord.

Romans 8:38–39

God's Unshakable Love

May the Lord awaken you to fresh and powerful
revelations of His love.

May He stir in you a deep desire to read His Word
and stand on His promises.

May He lift you up so you can see your life from His
perspective.

May He put a joy in your heart that makes you glad
and others smile.

And tonight, may you wrap yourself up in this wonderful truth: Absolutely nothing can separate you from
His love!

Sleep well.

There is no condemnation for those
who belong to Christ Jesus. And because
you belong to him, the power of the life-giving
Spirit has freed you from the power of sin
that leads to death. . . . The Spirit of God,
who raised Jesus from the dead, lives in you.
And just as God raised Christ Jesus from
the dead, he will give life to your
mortal bodies by this same Spirit
living within you.

Romans 8:1–2, 11

A Brand-New You

May God's opinion matter far more to you than man's
opinion.

May His dreams for you speak louder than your fears.

May His forgiveness wash over every sin from
your past.

And may you rise up in the morning with the
knowledge that He's made you brand-new,
through and through.

No spot or stain on you!

Rest well tonight.

You are my God,

and I will praise you;

you are my God,

and I will exalt you.

Give thanks to the LORD,

for he is good;

his love endures forever.

PSALM 118:28–29 NIV

The Lord's Goodness

May the Lord bless you with deep, nourishing sleep tonight.

May you wake up fresh and renewed, ready to face the day.

May you find the time to pause in His presence, listen for His voice, and give Him thanks for all He's done and for all He's about to do.

You are His beloved, and He is yours.

His banner over you is love!

Sleep well tonight.

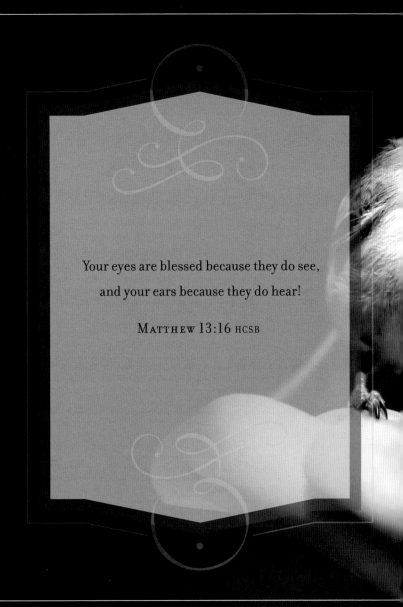

Your eyes are blessed because they do see,
and your ears because they do hear!

MATTHEW 13:16 HCSB

Seeing and Hearing God

May God bless your eyes so you begin to see everyone and everything redemptively.

May God bless your ears so you'll only hear words consistent with His voice and His song over your life.

May God bless your heart that you may be a wellspring of life for others.

And may God bless your hands and feet that you may tend to His business during your time on earth.

Your life matters deeply to Him.

Rest in that fact.

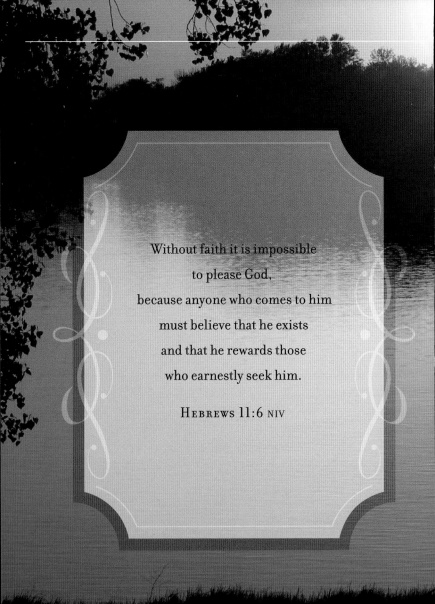

Without faith it is impossible
to please God,
because anyone who comes to him
must believe that he exists
and that he rewards those
who earnestly seek him.

HEBREWS 11:6 NIV

Heaven Is on Your Side

May you learn to trust God in increasing measures.

When He calls, may you follow where He leads, step out without having all of the information, speak up without having all the answers, and look up when your circumstances threaten to weigh you down.

May you live, breathe, and speak as one who is ensured victory and equipped to do the impossible.

Sleep well tonight, knowing that all of heaven is on your side.

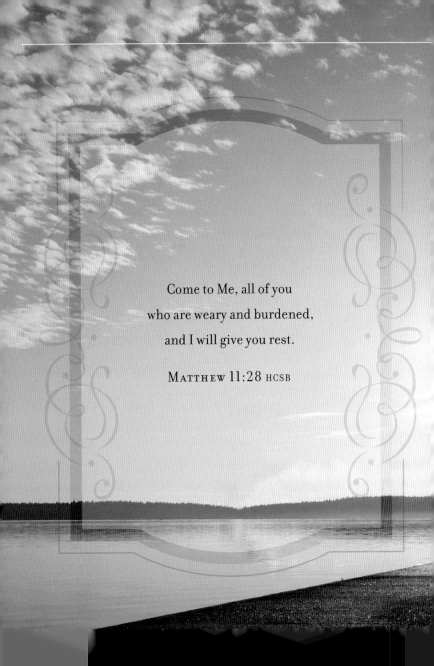

Come to Me, all of you
who are weary and burdened,
and I will give you rest.

MATTHEW 11:28 HCSB

A Healthy Rhythm

May the Lord establish in you a healthy, divine rhythm of life.

May He strengthen you in mind, body, and spirit.

Where you're broken, may He restore; where you're weary, may He refresh; where you're fearful, may He revive faith.

May your coming days be far more blessed than your former days.

Sleep well tonight. There will be new mercies waiting for you in the morning.

Remember this:
Whoever sows sparingly
will also reap sparingly,
and whoever sows generously
will also reap generously.
Each of you should give what you
have decided in your heart to give,
not reluctantly or under compulsion,
for God loves a cheerful giver.

2 Corinthians 9:6–7 niv

Sowing and Reaping

May God give you faith to sow seeds.

May you become a purposeful, generous, faith-filled sower.

May He
supply and increase
your store of seed and enlarge
the harvest of your righteousness.

May you be made rich in every way, generous in
every occasion, and leave the world thanking God for
your faithful soul!

Rest well tonight, knowing your Father in heaven possesses all.

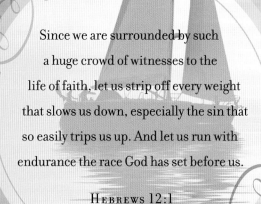

Since we are surrounded by such
a huge crowd of witnesses to the
life of faith, let us strip off every weight
that slows us down, especially the sin that
so easily trips us up. And let us run with
endurance the race God has set before us.

Hebrews 12:1

Stepping Out

May God inspire you to achieve a goal that He puts in your heart.

May He stir up faith as you step up and step out.

May He give you fresh conviction and discipline to say no to lesser things so you can say yes to His best plan for you.

May the wind of the Holy Spirit fill your sail and take you to a new, inspired place.

And tonight, sleep well.

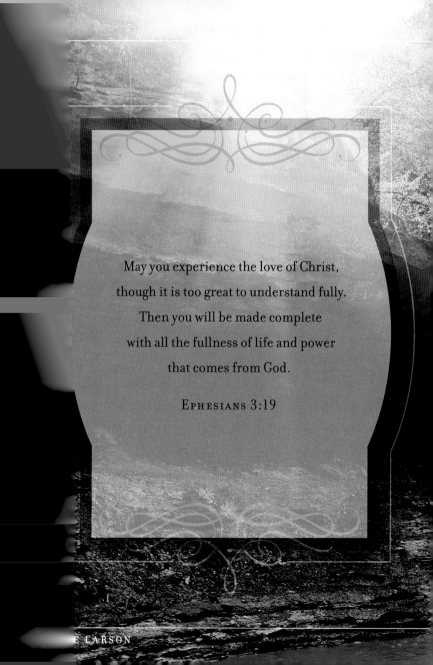

May you experience the love of Christ,
though it is too great to understand fully.
Then you will be made complete
with all the fullness of life and power
that comes from God.

EPHESIANS 3:19

E LARSON

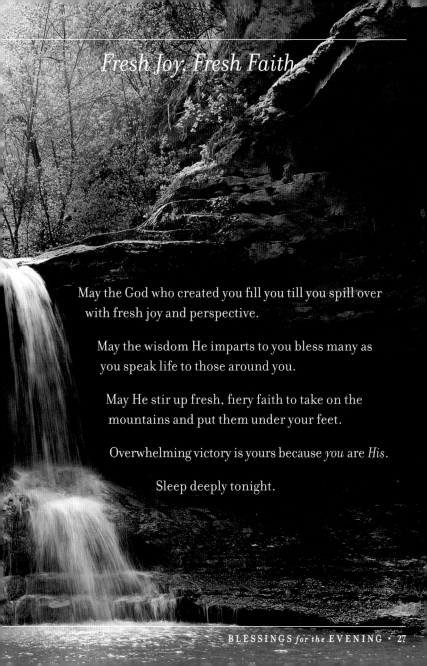

Fresh Joy, Fresh Faith

May the God who created you fill you till you spill over
with fresh joy and perspective.

May the wisdom He imparts to you bless many as
you speak life to those around you.

May He stir up fresh, fiery faith to take on the
mountains and put them under your feet.

Overwhelming victory is yours because *you* are *His*.

Sleep deeply tonight.

Praise the LORD, my soul; all my inmost being, praise his holy name. Praise the LORD, my soul, and forget not all his benefits—who forgives all your sins and heals all your diseases, who redeems your life from the pit and crowns you with love and compassion, who satisfies your desires with good things so that your youth is renewed like the eagle's.

PSALM 103:1–5 NIV

A Renewed Life

May the Lord dig up the stones
of pain, regret, and angst from your
soil and deliver you once and for all.

May He turn over the soil of your heart
and plant new seeds of faith, vision,
and purpose specific to your life's calling.

May He heal those deep places that nag you.

May He strengthen those weak places that leave you
feeling vulnerable.

And may He overwhelm you with a fresh revelation of His love so
you can believe that *nothing* is impossible with God on your side!

Sleep well tonight.

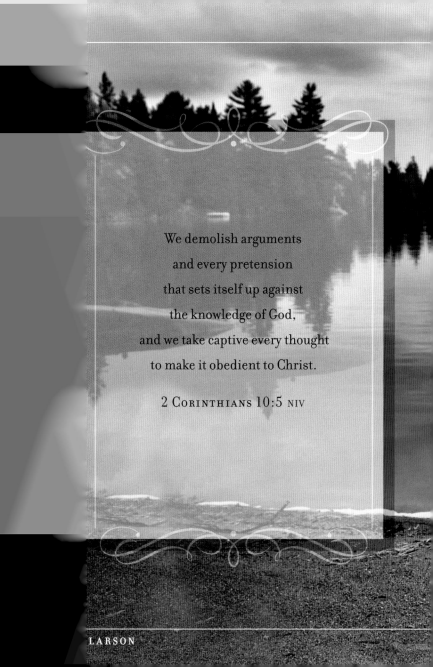

We demolish arguments
and every pretension
that sets itself up against
the knowledge of God,
and we take captive every thought
to make it obedient to Christ.

2 Corinthians 10:5 NIV

Christ in Focus

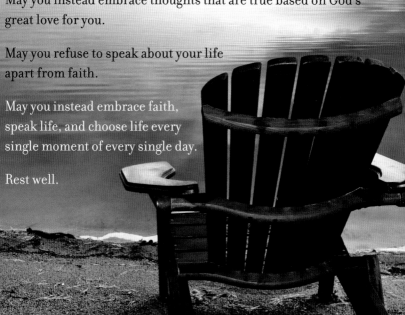

May God help you renew your mind and redeem your words.

May you refuse thoughts that weaken you, thoughts that take your eyes off of God.

May you instead embrace thoughts that are true based on God's great love for you.

May you refuse to speak about your life apart from faith.

May you instead embrace faith, speak life, and choose life every single moment of every single day.

Rest well.

The LORD

will fight for you;

you need only

to be still.

EXODUS 14:14 NIV

The Battle Is the Lord's

As you lie down to sleep, may the Lord himself rise up and fight for you!

May He draw by His Spirit your loved ones who do not love Him.

May He bring the breakthrough where there's only been a roadblock.

May you remember this day and every day that the battle is the Lord's!

Rest, knowing God fights for you!

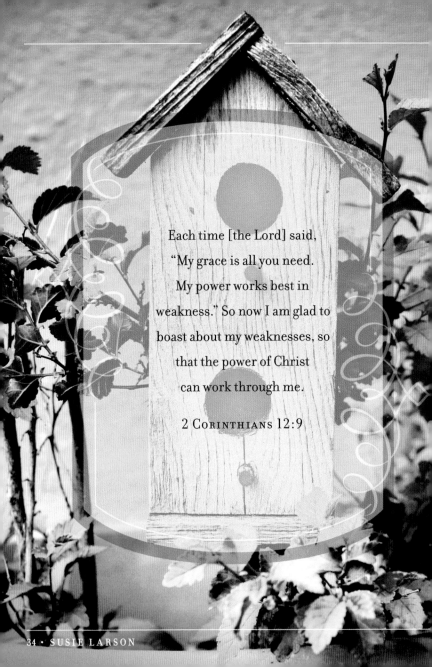

Each time [the Lord] said,
"My grace is all you need.
My power works best in
weakness." So now I am glad to
boast about my weaknesses, so
that the power of Christ
can work through me.

2 CORINTHIANS 12:9

Abounding Grace

May you—in spite of your mistakes and
missteps—see how God's love and provision
more than cover you.

May you—in your weakness—experience
abounding grace that makes you
divinely strong.

Where you've experienced loss and
brokenness, may you know healing,
wholeness, and redemption.

Your Redeemer is for you and He is strong.

Sleep well tonight.

My sheep listen to my voice;

I know them,

and they follow me.

John 10:27

Hearing God's Voice

May God give you Spirit-eyes to see the blessing in your battles.

May He give you Spirit-ears to hear His voice above all others.

May He give you a heart of faith to cling to His promises instead of your fears.

May you refuse to live beneath your spiritual privilege and instead live the other-worldly life He has offered you. You are so precious to Him!

Rest in His promises.

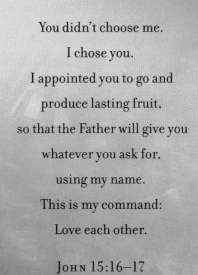

You didn't choose me.

I chose you.

I appointed you to go and

produce lasting fruit,

so that the Father will give you

whatever you ask for,

using my name.

This is my command:

Love each other.

John 15:16–17

An Eternal Perspective

As you wrap up your day, may God grace you with an eternal perspective.

Where there's only been disappointment, may you trust God's divine appointment and timing.

Where there's been discouragement, may He inspire new courage to stand strong.

Where there's been whining and griping, may you find a new song to sing and new reasons for thanksgiving.

May He break through the clouds so you'll see just how blessed you are.

Sleep well.

Unless the LORD builds the house,

the builders labor in vain.

Unless the LORD watches over the city,

the guards stand watch in vain.

In vain you rise early

and stay up late,

toiling for food to eat—

for he grants sleep to

those he loves.

PSALM 127:1–2 NIV

Love in Action

May the Lord bring fulfillment to your work, hilarity to your play,
depth to your prayers, and kindness to your words.

May He inspire perspective, conviction, and compassion
to change the world.

And tonight, may He grant blessed and sweet sleep.

If God is for us,

who can be against us?

He who did not spare his own Son,

but gave him up for us all—

how will he not also, along with him,

graciously give us all things? . . .

No, in all these things

we are more than conquerors

through him who loved us.

ROMANS 8:31–32, 37 NIV

Gritty Faith

May the Lord himself establish you in His best purposes for you.

May He strengthen you with holy conviction and gritty faith to climb every mountain He's assigned to you.

May He increase your capacity to love and encourage others.

And when the enemy rises up against you, may you see with your own eyes how God fights for you.

You're on the winning side.

You can rest.

The Lord is my shepherd;

I have all that I need.

He lets me rest in green meadows;

he leads me beside peaceful streams.

He renews my strength.

He guides me along right paths, bringing

honor to his name.

Psalm 23:1–3

Rest for the Weary

May God lead you beside still waters and provide rest
for your weary soul.

May He set you right where you're thinking is wrong.

May He give you faith to embrace the *you*
He's making you to be.

And may He give you wisdom to stand and fight when
your promised land depends on it.

You have everything you need in Him.

May God's rich blessings be yours tonight.

"No weapon forged against you
will prevail,
and you will refute every tongue
that accuses you.
This is the heritage of the servants
of the LORD,
and this is their vindication from me,"
declares the LORD.

ISAIAH 54:17 NIV

Equipped for Victory

(Speak this over yourself)

I am loved, called, and chosen.

I am rich in every way and generous on every occasion.

I'm anointed, appointed, equipped, and enabled by the power of God that works mightily within me! No weapon formed against me will prosper and no enemy scheme against me will succeed.

I live, breathe, and serve powerfully under the shelter of the Most High God. Amen.

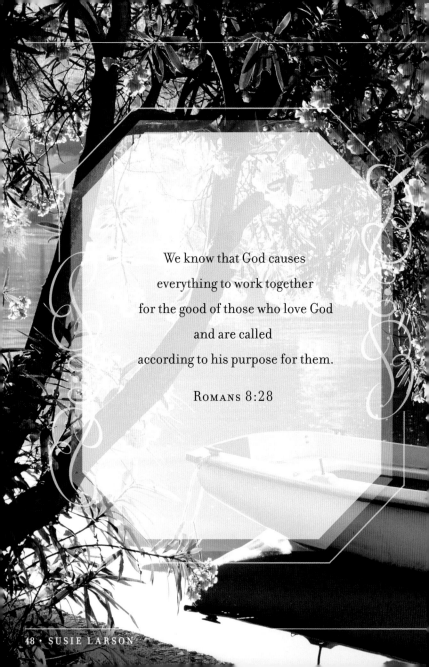

We know that God causes
everything to work together
for the good of those who love God
and are called
according to his purpose for them.

ROMANS 8:28

God Is Working for You

As the day draws to a close, may
you embrace God's grace,
trusting He'll fill every gap.

Instead of being unsettled
by your imperfections, may
you be undone by Jesus' perfect love for you.

Instead of fretting over your missteps,
rejoice that He never left your side today.

Scoop this day into your hand and lift it up as an offering to the
One who moves mountains and ministers miracles with every
little handful we give Him.

He's a miracle-working God and He loves you.

I have not stopped thanking God for you.

I pray for you constantly,

asking God, the glorious Father

of our Lord Jesus Christ,

to give you spiritual wisdom

and insight so that

you might grow in

your knowledge of God.

EPHESIANS 1:16–17

A Personal Revival

May you experience a personal revival that forever marks the way you walk with God.

May your loved ones encounter Him in ways that change how they pray, what they say, and how they live.

May God move on your prayers in ways that compel you to pray more specifically, with greater fervency, and with increasing faith.

Though the enemy is working over-time, he runs scared when God steps in.

May God move mightily in our midst in the days ahead!

Have a blessed and faith-filled evening!

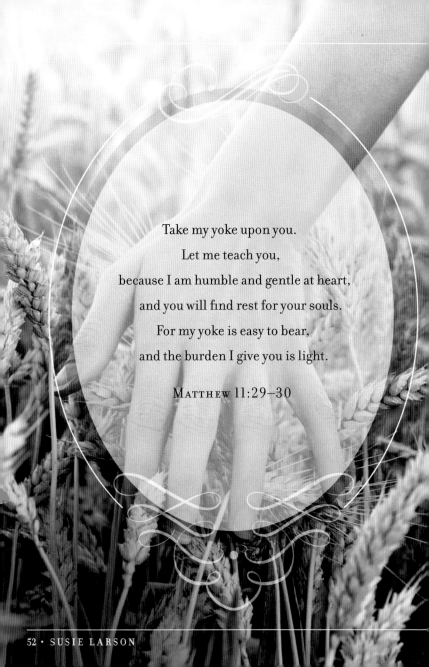

Take my yoke upon you.

Let me teach you,

because I am humble and gentle at heart,

and you will find rest for your souls.

For my yoke is easy to bear,

and the burden I give you is light.

MATTHEW 11:29–30

Let God Carry the Load

May you have the presence of mind to cherish every second with the ones you love.

May you make time for fun, for rest, and for reflection.

May you plan time in your schedule not to have plans, and see what happens.

May you come to know—on a whole new level—that much more rests on God's shoulders than on yours.

And may you learn to enjoy the journey because His yoke is easy and His burden is light.

And He's crazy in love with you.

Sleep well tonight.

He will cover you
with his feathers.
He will shelter you
with his wings.
His faithful promises are
your armor and protection.

PSALM 91:4

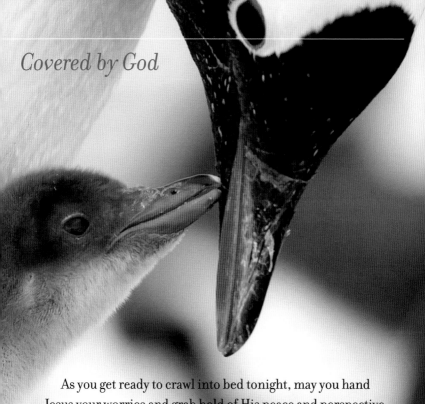

Covered by God

As you get ready to crawl into bed tonight, may you hand Jesus your worries and grab hold of His peace and perspective.

May you lay down your judgments and hold close His fresh mercies.

As you slip under the covers, remember you're not under your circumstances, you are under the shadow of His wings.

Take hold of what you possess in Him, and sleep well.

So shall they fear the name of the LORD
from the west,
and His glory from the rising of the sun;
when the enemy comes in like a flood,
the Spirit of the LORD will lift up
a standard against him.

ISAIAH 59:19 NKJV

Coming Against the Enemy

May God give you faith to put fear under your feet.

May you know that for every way the enemy comes against you,
the Lord has a promise to bless you to help you stand strong.

May you fix your eyes on Jesus and set your heart on His Word.

Know this: When the enemy comes in like a flood, the Lord will
raise up a standard against him!

Trust in God and sleep in peace tonight.

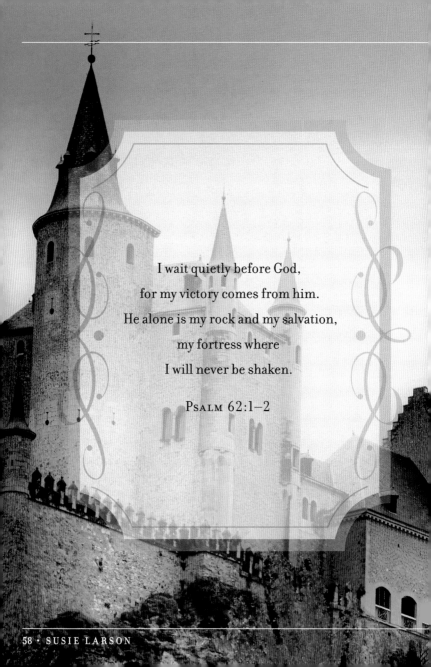

I wait quietly before God,
for my victory comes from him.
He alone is my rock and my salvation,
my fortress where
I will never be shaken.

PSALM 62:1–2

He Is Faithful

May God open the heavens, break through the clouds, and deliver the answer you've been waiting for.

May He shore up your faith, strengthen your heart, and overwhelm you with His grace.

May your soul know a peaceful assurance like it's never known before.

May you believe from deep within that God is with you, for you, and will never let you go.

He is mighty to save.

Rest well tonight.

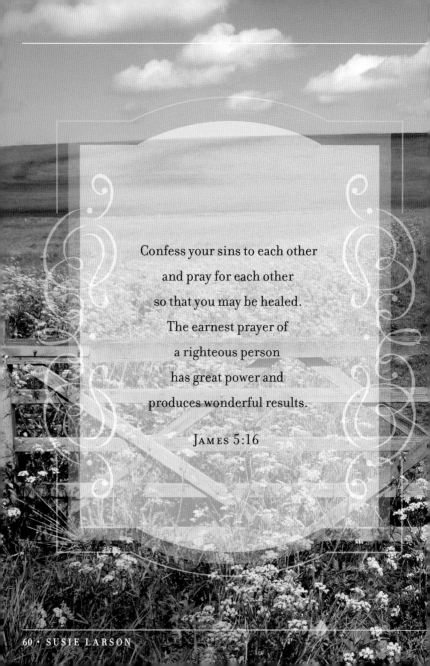

Confess your sins to each other
and pray for each other
so that you may be healed.
The earnest prayer of
a righteous person
has great power and
produces wonderful results.

JAMES 5:16

Right Place, Right Time

May God stir up fresh faith in your heart.

May your prayers be packed with power and your words seasoned with love.

May God give you divine instinct so you're always in the right place at the right time.

And may He open a door for you no man can close.

Sleep deeply, sleep well!

As for God, his way is perfect:

The LORD's word is flawless;

he shields all who take refuge in him.

For who is God besides the LORD?

And who is the Rock except our God?

It is God who arms me with strength

and keeps my way secure.

He makes my feet like the feet of a deer;

he causes me to stand on the heights.

2 SAMUEL 22:31–34 NIV

The Rock

May God's love and truth bring clarity and purpose to your life.

May His strength steady your steps.

May His compassion open your eyes and may His conviction make your heart beat strong.

May His kingdom come and His will be done in and through you.

Rest in His truth.

May the God of your father help you;

may the Almighty bless you with

the blessings of the heavens above,

and blessings of the watery depths below,

and blessings of the breasts and womb.

May the blessings of your father surpass

the blessings of the ancient mountains,

reaching to the heights of the eternal hills.

May these blessings rest on the head of Joseph,

who is a prince among his brothers.

GENESIS 49:25–26

Grateful Living

May you wrap your arms around the ones you love,
look them in the eyes, and tell them
how much you treasure them.

May you look around and take notice
of all the blessings you'd miss
if they went away tomorrow.

When you're tempted to indulge in
melancholy or discontentment, may
you instead jump up, raise your hands,
and thank God for His daily and divine
intervention in your life.

May your humble gratitude give you keen
spiritual insight and restful peace.

May all who fear you
find in me a cause for joy,
for I have put my hope
in your word.

PSALM 119:74

From Fearful to Joyful

May God surround you with His tender mercies and encompass you with a fresh revelation of His love.

May He keep you hidden away from toxic people and strengthen your healthy relationships.

May He bless you with a new friend who sees what He sees in you.

And may you rest tonight knowing He'll be there to greet you in the morning.

Sleep deeply, sleep well.

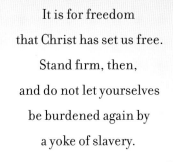

It is for freedom
that Christ has set us free.
Stand firm, then,
and do not let yourselves
be burdened again by
a yoke of slavery.

GALATIANS 5:1 NIV

Freedom in Christ

It is *for* freedom that Christ has set you free.

May you refuse to be subject to any yoke of slavery—slavery to sin, fear, legalism, or striving.

May you rest in the knowledge that Jesus paid it all
 so that you could walk free and whole.

May you boldly live the abundant, fruitful life
He had in mind from the beginning.

You are everything to Him.

It is good to give thanks to the LORD,

to sing praises to the Most High.

It is good to proclaim your unfailing love

in the morning, your faithfulness in

the evening.... You thrill me, LORD,

with all you have done for me!

I sing for joy because of

what you have done.

PSALM 92:1–2, 4

Praises to the Most High

May you raise your arms and praise God for His faithfulness to you.

May you open your hands and receive what He so lovingly wants to give.

May you look past your circumstances and see Jesus who reigns over all.

And may you move forward in faith, knowing all things are possible through Him.

A blessed and restful night to you!

I don't mean to say that I have already achieved these things or that I have already reached perfection. But I press on to possess that perfection for which Christ Jesus first possessed me. No, dear brothers and sisters, I have not achieved it, but I focus on this one thing: Forgetting the past and looking forward to what lies ahead, I press on to reach the end of the race and receive the heavenly prize for which God, through Christ Jesus, is calling us.

PHILIPPIANS 3:12–14

A Heavenly Aim

May you embrace the grace to leave your past in God's hands.

May you have the grit to face down your fears.

May you have the gumption to go after your God-given dreams.

And may you see God's glory shining over every part of your life.

He gives good gifts to His children.

Rest well tonight.

But the godly will flourish
like palm trees and grow strong
like the cedars of Lebanon.
For they are transplanted to
the Lord's own house.
They flourish in the courts
of our God.
Even in old age they will
still produce fruit;
they will remain vital and green.

Psalm 92:12–14

A Fruitful Life

May you walk with a new confidence that in Christ you are prized, loved, accepted, called, equipped, and sent out to change the world.

You lack no good thing!

And tonight, may you rest in His shadow. He's got you.

But as for me,

it is good to be near God.

I have made the Sovereign Lord

my refuge;

I will tell of all your deeds.

Psalm 73:28 NIV

Step-by-Step With God

May God surround you with a strong sense of
His great love for you!

May you live every day with the expectancy
that He is moving in your life.

May the Word of God come alive to you in a
way you've never experienced.

And may your prayers take on a whole new level of
power and faith.

You are His child and He is with you every step of the way.

Be blessed with deep rest this evening.

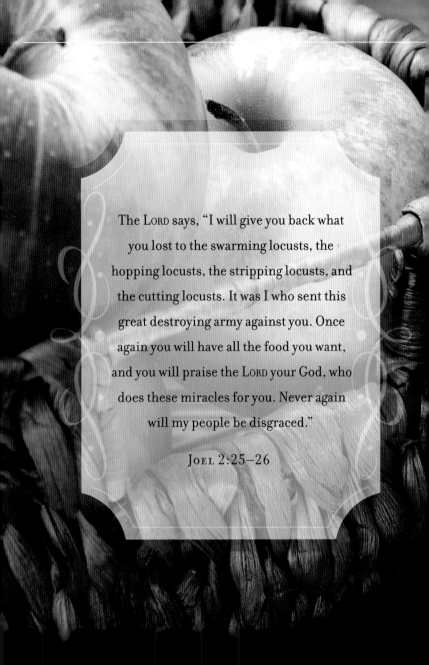

The LORD says, "I will give you back what you lost to the swarming locusts, the hopping locusts, the stripping locusts, and the cutting locusts. It was I who sent this great destroying army against you. Once again you will have all the food you want, and you will praise the LORD your God, who does these miracles for you. Never again will my people be disgraced."

JOEL 2:25–26

Your New Future

May God lift you up and heal and restore you fully.

May you see glimpses of His glory everywhere you turn.

May He show you wonders of His love that overwhelm
you and make your knees weak.

May He put a new song in your heart and a new dream
in your spirit.

May you walk forward unafraid and full of faith
that your future will be far greater than
your past.

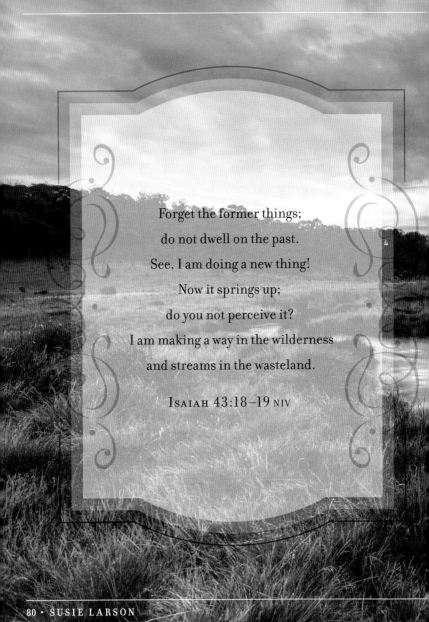

Forget the former things;

do not dwell on the past.

See, I am doing a new thing!

Now it springs up;

do you not perceive it?

I am making a way in the wilderness

and streams in the wasteland.

ISAIAH 43:18–19 NIV

A Mighty Move of God

May you have a strong sense of the impossible things God wants
to do in, through, and around you.

May God's dream for you swallow up your unbelief!

May you have faith enough to
put out your buckets and
prepare for rain.

God moves on faith. May He move mightily
because of yours.

And tonight, enjoy restful, faith-filled sleep.

God is mighty to save.

Teach us
to number our days,
that we may gain
a heart of wisdom.

Psalm 90:12 NIV

Sacred Moments

May God help you be fully present with the ones you love.

May He give you discernment not to pass by the sacred moments He supplies.

May He give you faith to believe Him for great things and insight to fully embrace what you already possess in Him.

And may He overwhelm you with a renewed sense of His very personal love for you.

Sleep well tonight.

Don't be afraid—you're not going to be embarrassed. Don't hold back—you're not going to come up short. You'll forget all about the humiliations of your youth, and the indignities of being a widow will fade from memory. For your Maker is your bridegroom, his name, God-of-the-Angel-Armies! Your Redeemer is The Holy of Israel, known as God of the whole earth.

ISAIAH 54:4–5 THE MESSAGE

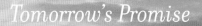

Tomorrow's Promise

May God expand your territory, enlarge your
vision, and increase your capacity for His
influence in your life.

May you be quick to hear, quick to obey, and quick to
trust Him with every detail of your life.

As you consider His faithfulness today, may you walk
faithfully to your next place of promise tomorrow.

He has been faithful. He *will* be faithful.

Rest assured of that.

Through followers of Jesus like yourselves gathered in churches, this extraordinary plan of God is becoming known and talked about even among the angels! All this is proceeding along lines planned all along by God and then executed in Christ Jesus. When we trust in him, we're free to say whatever needs to be said, bold to go wherever we need to go.

Ephesians 3:10–12 The Message

Secure in Christ

May you understand on a greater
level your secure standing in Christ.

May you approach Him with fresh
boldness and faith, assured of His glad
welcome.

May your prayers move heaven and earth, and
may you remember that everywhere you place your
feet, God's kingdom comes to earth.

GOD made my life complete when I placed
all the pieces before him. When I got my
act together, he gave me a fresh start.
Now I'm alert to GOD's ways; I don't take
God for granted. Every day I review the
ways he works; I try not to miss a trick.
I feel put back together, and I'm watching
my step. GOD rewrote the text of my life
when I opened the book of my heart
to his eyes.

PSALM 18:20–24 THE MESSAGE

Living With Expectancy

Jesus is coming soon.

May God open your eyes to see the reality of His kingdom in your midst, may He open your ears that you may clearly hear His voice, and may He awaken your heart that you may passionately and purposefully live for Him.

Live expectantly and sleep well.

If you then, being evil,
know how to give good gifts
to your children, how much more
will your heavenly Father
give the Holy Spirit to
those who ask Him!

LUKE 11:13 NKJV

Good Gifts

May you slow down long enough tomorrow to enjoy the sacredness of the present moment.

May God give you plenty of sacred pauses to reflect on His intimate and powerful love for you.

May you enjoy lots of face-to-face encounters with those you love.

May God open your eyes and use you to lift up those bent beneath heavy loads.

May *you* receive the gifts He so lovingly wants to give.

And tonight, may you enjoy deep, refreshing sleep.

Tomorrow's a new day.

I cry out to God Most High,

to God, who vindicates me.

He sends from heaven and saves me,

rebuking those who hotly pursue me—

God sends forth his love and

his faithfulness.

PSALM 57:2–3 NIV

Mighty to Save

May the Lord continue to fight for you while you rest in Him.

May He confuse the enemy's schemes against you.

May He surround you with God-fearing, faithful friends and strengthen your resolve to live courageously.

You're on the winning side!

Sleep well.

Since God chose you to be the holy people he loves, you must clothe yourselves with tenderhearted mercy, kindness, humility, gentleness, and patience. Make allowance for each other's faults, and forgive anyone who offends you. Remember, the Lord forgave you, so you must forgive others. Above all, clothe yourselves with love, which binds us all together in perfect harmony. And let the peace that comes from Christ rule in your hearts. For as members of one body you are called to live in peace. And always be thankful.

Colossians 3:12–15

A Peace Offering

May God give you kindness and grace for those who step on your toes.

May He give you holy and humble confidence in the presence of those who misunderstand you.

May He give you love and forgiveness for those who hurt you and grace for those who miss you completely.

And may His love spill over you till you know that you are everything to Him.

Sleep well tonight. Walk confidently tomorrow.

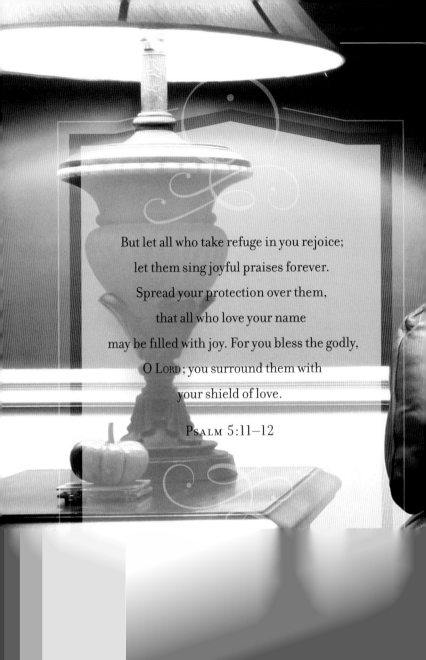

But let all who take refuge in you rejoice;

let them sing joyful praises forever.

Spread your protection over them,

that all who love your name

may be filled with joy. For you bless the godly,

O Lord; you surround them with

your shield of love.

Psalm 5:11–12

A Shield of Love

As the day draws to a close and your body gets ready to rest, may your soul awaken to the wonder of God's movement in your life.

He is with you and for you.

His love and favor surround you like a shield.

Listen to His voice as you rest your head on the pillow tonight.

Forsake your worries and fears and cling to faith instead. He's got you in His hands.

Don't worry about anything;

instead, pray about everything.

Tell God what you need,

and thank him for all he has done.

Then you will experience God's peace,

which exceeds anything

we can understand.

His peace will guard your hearts and

minds as you live in Christ Jesus.

PHILIPPIANS 4:6–7

A Thankful Heart

May you set aside your fears, worries, and frustrations,
and pull close the ones you love.

May you notice and give thanks for all that is right
in your world.

May the Lord become especially real to you
in the coming days.

And may you grow in your capacity to thank Him
and trust Him in every single circumstance.

Enjoy sweet rest tonight.

Always be full of joy in the Lord.

I say it again—rejoice!

Let everyone see that you

are considerate in all you do.

Remember, the Lord is coming soon.

Philippians 4:4–5

Your Story and God's

May you grow to love and accept the *you*
God is making you to be.

May you walk in a new level of grace and
gratitude that gives you peace and leaves
others encouraged.

May you be more apt to look forward with
hope than you are to look back with regret.

May your heart spill over
with joy at the very
thought of the story
God is writing with
your life.

Rest in His love.

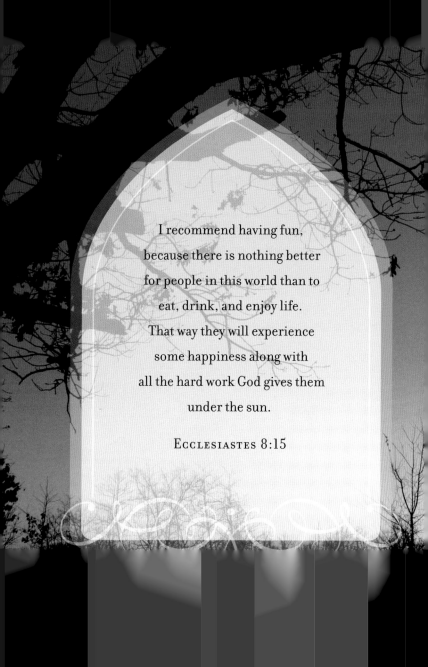

I recommend having fun,
because there is nothing better
for people in this world than to
eat, drink, and enjoy life.
That way they will experience
some happiness along with
all the hard work God gives them
under the sun.

Ecclesiastes 8:15

A Full-of-Life Life

May God surprise you with moments of grace and refreshment.

May He bring the long-awaited breakthrough.

May He bless you with sudden belly laughter and watery-eyed joy.

May He give you a gift that you least expect.

And may He inspire you to pray more audaciously than you ever have before.

He is with you and for you.

Be joyful in hope,

patient in affliction,

faithful in prayer.

ROMANS 12:12 NIV

Through God's Eyes

May God give you His perspective on the things
that frustrate you.

May your heart of compassion grow for those
who suffer in unimaginable ways.

May you pray as passionately for them
as you do for yourself.

May God protect you from a small, selfish mind-set.

May He fill you up with thanksgiving and joy for the
freedoms you enjoy!

May He renew your resolve to be a
grateful, humble soul.

And may He use you tomorrow in
ways that surprise and bless you.

Sweet dreams.

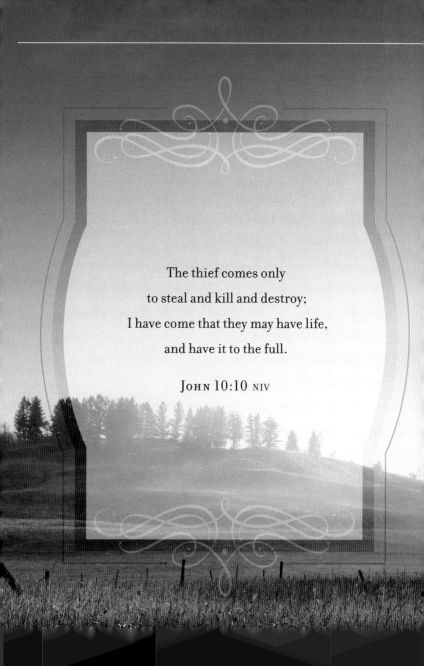

The thief comes only
to steal and kill and destroy;
I have come that they may have life,
and have it to the full.

JOHN 10:10 NIV

Fully Restored

May God himself restore to you something you lost and never thought you'd get back again.

May He heal a soul wound you thought you'd never get over.

May He pour out an abundance of joy and hope that makes you celebrate before the answer comes.

And may a thriving, rich faith mark your life in every way.

You have access to the Most High God. May you live accordingly.

Rest easy tonight!

The LORD is gracious and righteous;

our God is full of compassion.

The LORD protects the unwary;

when I was brought low,

he saved me.

Return to your rest, my soul,

for the LORD has been good to you.

PSALM 116:5–7 NIV

While You Rest

May God work mightily tonight while you rest.

May He move mountains on your behalf.

May He part the waters so you can pass through to
your next place of promise.

May you grow in the knowledge of God's love and become a flow-
through-account of His blessings to a world in need.

Sleep well tonight.

Don't you realize that in a race everyone runs,
but only one person gets the prize?
So run to win! All athletes are disciplined in
their training. They do it to win a prize that will
fade away, but we do it for an eternal prize.
So I run with purpose in every step.
I am not just shadowboxing. I discipline my
body like an athlete, training it to do what it
should. Otherwise, I fear that after preaching to
others I myself might be disqualified.

1 Corinthians 9:24–27

Purpose in Every Step

May God establish you in His highest and best purposes for you.

May He point out your time-wasters and life-drainers,
and may you have the grit to walk away from them.

May His passion become your passion so that your life
reflects His abundant life plan for you.

And tonight, may your sleep heal and restore you
in every way.

You're treasured and blessed.

Then, because so many people
were coming and going that
they did not even have a chance to eat,
[Jesus] said to them, "Come with me
by yourselves to a quiet place
and get some rest."

MARK 6:31 NIV

A Quiet Place

May you put a high priority on rest and replenishment.

May you make a plan to get away and nourish your soul.

May you do your work with great excellence.

May you take on a challenge that stretches your faith
and increases your dependence on God.

May your work be especially satisfying and
your rest be especially sweet.

Life is good that way.

Bless you!

Let us hold unswervingly
to the hope we profess,
for he who promised
is faithful.

HEBREWS 10:23 NIV

A Better Tomorrow

May you find a moment of peace and quiet tonight to
thank God for all that is right in your world.

May you have the presence of
mind to release your cares
and worries to Him.

May you have the gritty faith
to grab a firmer grip on
His promises to you.

And may you wake up in the morning knowing that
you've gained ground even during your sleeping
hours because God is always moving on your behalf.

As you entrust your whole self to Him today,
He'll get you where you need to go tomorrow.

He is faithful.

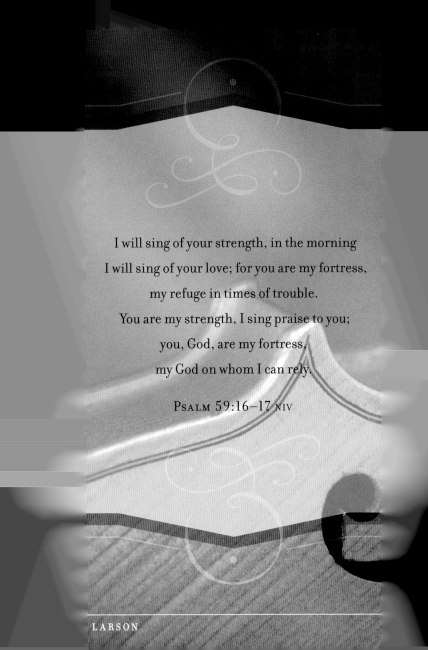

I will sing of your strength, in the morning
I will sing of your love; for you are my fortress,
my refuge in times of trouble.
You are my strength, I sing praise to you;
you, God, are my fortress,
my God on whom I can rely.

Psalm 59:16–17 NIV

LARSON

You Can Rely on Him

God is your creator, defender, deliverer, and provider.

May He inspire fresh, creative ways to make a living.

May He defend you against the accusations of your critics.

May He deliver you from the schemes of the enemy.

And may He more than provide for all your needs.

He is faithful.

Sleep well in that assurance.

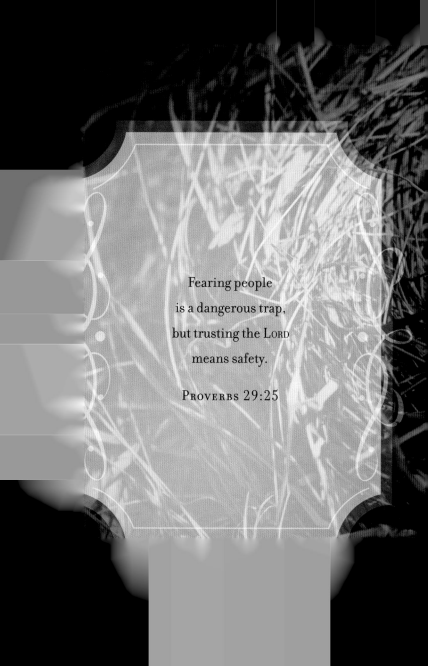

Fearing people
is a dangerous trap,
but trusting the LORD
means safety.

PROVERBS 29:25

Fearing God, Not Man

May you be
content to know that
you cannot be all things to all
people; you live to serve an audience of One.

May you love people but keep your hope in God.

May you be willing to take risks with people, but may your sole
trust be in God.

May the power you once gave to others rest solely on God because
He defines, He saves, He provides, and He has the power to
transform.

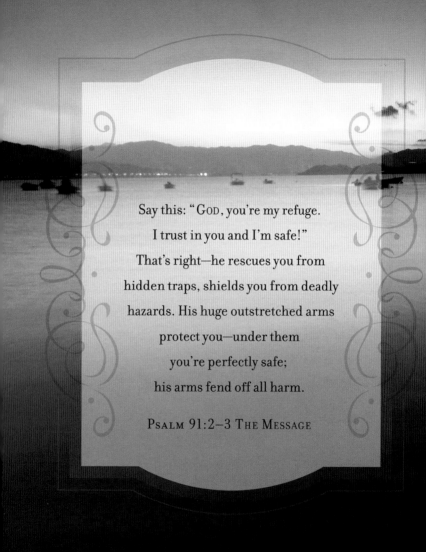

Say this: "GOD, you're my refuge.
I trust in you and I'm safe!"
That's right—he rescues you from
hidden traps, shields you from deadly
hazards. His huge outstretched arms
protect you—under them
you're perfectly safe;
his arms fend off all harm.

PSALM 91:2–3 THE MESSAGE

Following His Lead

May you have the wisdom to run away from temptation
and into the arms of God.

May you know when to run to the battlefield and
when to hide in His shadow.

May you have the courage to run up the mountain and the
guts to step out of the boat when it is required of you.

May your every step be in step with Him.

Sleep well.

Even before he made the world,

God loved us and chose us

in Christ to be holy

and without fault in his eyes.

EPHESIANS 1:4

God Is for You

May God remove every hindrance that keeps you
from knowing His love in a way that changes you.

May He change every circumstance that sends a lying
message to you.

May He highlight every trial He's using to train you
into a warrior.

And may He remind you that all of heaven is on your side.

You are very close to His heart.

Rest in that fact.

Dear friend, I pray that you
may enjoy good health and that
all may go well with you, even as your
soul is getting along well. It gave me great
joy when some believers came and testified
about your faithfulness to the truth,
telling how you continue to walk in it.

3 John 1:2–3 NIV

Abundant Living and Giving

May God prosper you in every way.

May you be emotionally strong and stable,
spiritually deep and thriving, financially free
and generous, socially blessed and a blessing,
and physically fit and healthy.

May God fill in every gap, heal every wound,
and restore everything stolen.

May you live abundantly in every way.

And may you sleep well tonight.

Now he who supplies seed to the sower
and bread for food will also supply and
increase your store of seed and will enlarge the
harvest of your righteousness.
You will be enriched in every way
so that you can be generous on every occasion,
and through us your generosity will result
in thanksgiving to God.

2 CORINTHIANS 9:10–11 NIV

Harvest Time

May you sow the seeds God has given
you to sow.

May you reap above and beyond anything you
could ever ask or think.

May you know without a doubt your divine call.

And may you open your arms wide and receive
everything God provides along the way.

Have a restful night.

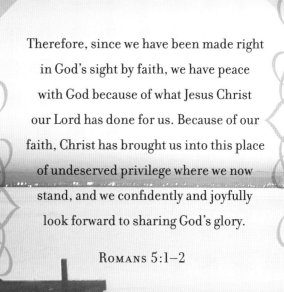

Therefore, since we have been made right
in God's sight by faith, we have peace
with God because of what Jesus Christ
our Lord has done for us. Because of our
faith, Christ has brought us into this place
of undeserved privilege where we now
stand, and we confidently and joyfully
look forward to sharing God's glory.

Romans 5:1–2

Valued

May you learn deeply just how important you are to God.

May you grasp your spiritual wealth and appropriate
your spiritual strength.

May your fears dissolve and your worries vaporize.

May you walk in the full assurance of God's love,
acceptance, and grace.

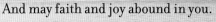

And may faith and joy abound in you.

Rest in Him.

The Scriptures . . . say,
"No eye has seen, no ear has heard,
and no mind has imagined what God
has prepared for those who love him."
But it was to us that God revealed
these things by his Spirit.
For his Spirit searches out everything
and shows us God's deep secrets.

1 Corinthians 2:9–10

Beyond Imagination

May you believe that your wildest God-given dreams
can come true.

May you trust Jesus enough to follow Him
through the valley to lay hold of them.

May you be patient and purposeful.

May your selfish ambition die and your
holy ambition arise.

May you lean into your training time so you'll
be strengthened and prepared to stand in your
next place of promise.

Then you'll be poised to change the world.

Tonight, sleep well.

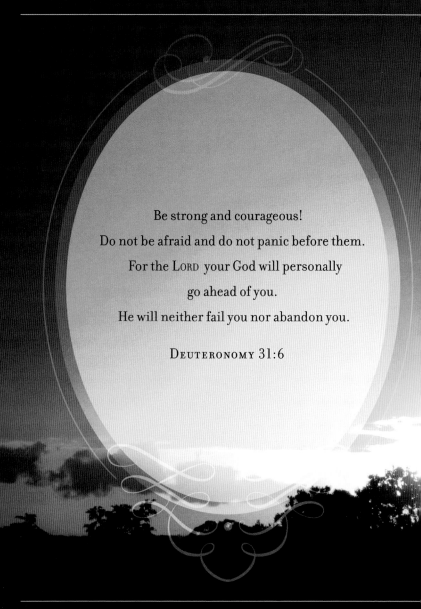

Be strong and courageous!
Do not be afraid and do not panic before them.
For the LORD your God will personally
go ahead of you.
He will neither fail you nor abandon you.

DEUTERONOMY 31:6

God Will Lead You

When you are tired and weary, may God give you rest and
a right perspective.

When you are tempted to run ahead on your own, may
He give you divine wisdom to wait on Him.

When your guard is down and you are vulnerable to the
enemy's schemes, may God protect you on every side
and deliver you.

And when you are ready to fly, may He lift you up
and bless you before a watching world.

Take one humble step at a time. He will lead you
to your next place
of promise.

May nourishing sleep
be yours.

Faith is the confidence
that what we hope for will
actually happen;
it gives us assurance
about things
we cannot see.

HEBREWS 11:1

Faith-Filled Eyes

May you choose to be grateful when you would rather be grumpy.

May you choose to rejoice in God's goodness when you are tempted to rehearse man's badness.

May you sing into your empty well, trusting that God will soon fill it.

And may you live with the expectancy that any day now, the Lord will bring the breakthrough.

Find peace tonight in the knowledge that more rests on God's shoulders than on yours. He's got you.

Good night!

I pray that from his glorious, unlimited resources he will empower you with inner strength through his Spirit. Then Christ will make his home in your hearts as you trust in him. Your roots will grow down into God's love and keep you strong. And may you have the power to understand, as all God's people should, how wide, how long, how high, and how deep his love is.

Ephesians 3:16–18

Rooted in Love

May God himself lift you up and make you strong.

May He intervene where you cannot.

May He shine His light on the enemy's schemes.

May He confuse the enemy's plans and profoundly answer your prayers.

May He establish you in His highest and best purposes for your life.

You matter deeply to Him.

Blessed sleep be yours tonight!

Patient endurance is what you need now,

so that you will continue

to do God's will.

Then you will receive all that

he has promised.

HEBREWS 10:36

Reaping Results

May your hard work reap exceptional rewards.

May your earnest prayers accomplish great and powerful things.

May your faith-filled gifts produce exponential results.

And may your rest heal and restore you in every way.

Sleep well tonight.

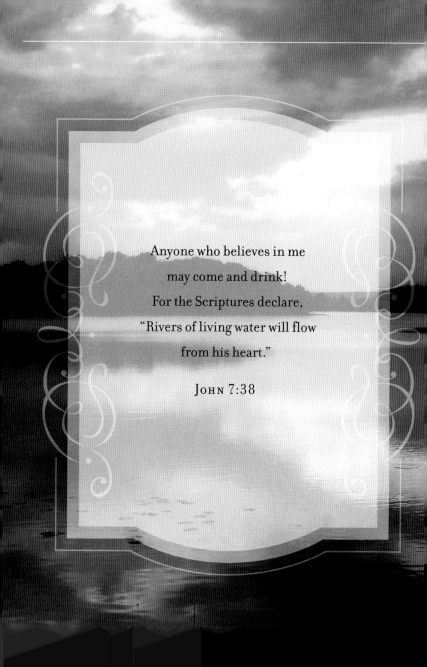

Anyone who believes in me
may come and drink!
For the Scriptures declare,
"Rivers of living water will flow
from his heart."

JOHN 7:38

Life-Giving Water

May God bless you with spontaneous fun and hilarious laughter.

May He break through in a sudden moment with a greater-than-expected answer.

May He bless you with Sabbath-moments of replenishment and rest.

And by God's grace may you impart life and healing to every conversation.

And tonight, sweet dreams.

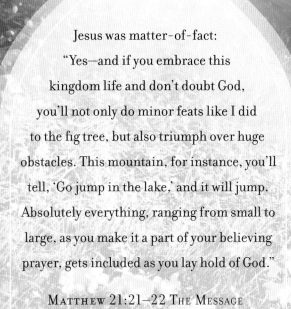

Jesus was matter-of-fact:
"Yes—and if you embrace this
kingdom life and don't doubt God,
you'll not only do minor feats like I did
to the fig tree, but also triumph over huge
obstacles. This mountain, for instance, you'll
tell, 'Go jump in the lake,' and it will jump.
Absolutely everything, ranging from small to
large, as you make it a part of your believing
prayer, gets included as you lay hold of God."

MATTHEW 21:21–22 THE MESSAGE

Facing Down Fears

May God pour out fresh grace where life's been a grind.

May He impart peace where you've only known pain.

May He release a mighty faith to face down your fears.

And because He is faithful, may you courageously take on the mountain in front of you.

But tonight, sleep well.

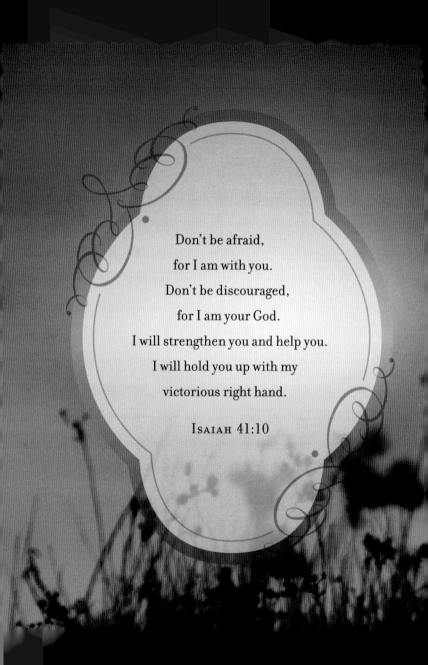

Don't be afraid,
for I am with you.
Don't be discouraged,
for I am your God.
I will strengthen you and help you.
I will hold you up with my
victorious right hand.

ISAIAH 41:10

Your Defender and Protector

May you stand strong in the face of your fears and stronger still when it comes to your faith.

May you bow low when you'd rather exalt yourself and bow lower still in the presence of God.

May you accept grace for your own missteps and offer more grace still when someone steps on you.

God is your defender and protector.

Trust in Him.

How great is the goodness you have stored up
for those who fear you. You lavish it on those
who come to you for protection,
blessing them before the watching world.
You hide them in the shelter of your presence,
safe from those who conspire against them.
You shelter them in your presence,
far from accusing tongues.

PSALM 31:19–20

Shelter in the Storm

May God draw you in so close that your heart beats
in rhythm with His.

May He keep you far from accusing tongues and critical spirits.

May He fill your ears with words of truth, direction,
promise, and love.

May your face shine with the strong assurance
that you belong to God.

You, Lᴏʀᴅ, hear the desire
of the afflicted;
you encourage them,
and you listen
to their cry.

Psᴀʟᴍ 10:17 ɴɪᴠ

Glimpses of Glory

May new breakthroughs be yours all around.

May you start to see glimpses of God's glory, tokens of your faith, and evidences that God is moving on your behalf.

May the winds start to blow, letting you know that answers to your heart's desires are on their way.

And tonight, may your sleep nourish your soul and restore your health.

Good night!

May the God who gives endurance
and encouragement give you the same
attitude of mind toward each other
that Christ Jesus had,
so that with one mind and one voice
you may glorify the God and
Father of our Lord Jesus Christ.

Romans 15:5–6 NIV

When You'd Rather . . .

May God grant you grace
when you'd rather grumble.

May He inspire hope
when you'd rather breathe a heavy sigh.

May He help you be kind
when you'd rather be cruel.

May you rest in Him tonight
and be more like Him
tomorrow.

I, a prisoner for serving the Lord,
beg you to lead a life worthy of your calling,
for you have been called by God.
Always be humble and gentle.
Be patient with each other, making allowance
for each other's faults because of your love.
Make every effort to keep yourselves united
in the Spirit, binding yourselves
together with peace.

EPHESIANS 4:1–3

United With Christ

May God heal your broken relationships, refresh your tired relationships, and sustain your new relationships.

May He awaken in you a new awareness of His presence and His love.

And may the quality and the power of your communion with Christ transform every aspect of your life.

And tonight, may you rest well in Him.

I pray that the eyes of your heart may be enlightened in order that you may know the hope to which he has called you, the riches of his glorious inheritance in his holy people, and his incomparably great power for us who believe. That power is the same as the mighty strength he exerted when he raised Christ from the dead and seated him at his right hand in the heavenly realms, far above all rule and authority, power and dominion, and every name that is invoked, not only in the present age but also in the one to come.

Ephesians 1:18–21 NIV

Incomparable Power

May your prayers be filled with power.

May your words be full of grace and truth.

May your God-given dreams surprise and inspire you.

And may your kindness and generosity change the world.

Sleep well. God is with you.

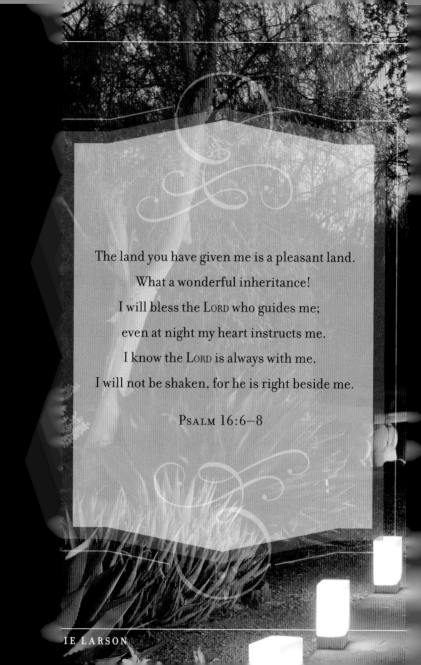

The land you have given me is a pleasant land.

What a wonderful inheritance!

I will bless the LORD who guides me;

even at night my heart instructs me.

I know the LORD is always with me.

I will not be shaken, for he is right beside me.

PSALM 16:6–8

IE LARSON

An Ever-Present Help

As the day wraps up and you crawl into bed tonight, may your body, mind, and soul be at rest and know the deep, abiding peace that comes from deeply knowing God.

May He speak to you while you sleep and may He download fresh insight and perspective regarding your current circumstances.

And as you rise up in the morning, may faith rise up in you and compel you to obey when you'd rather self-protect, give when you'd rather hoard, and trust when you're tempted to worry.

You're not made for this place. You're only passing through.

Live as one who is spoken for.

Good night!

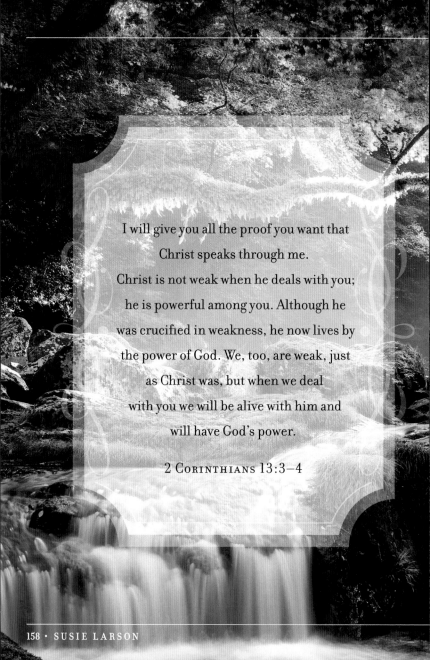

I will give you all the proof you want that
Christ speaks through me.
Christ is not weak when he deals with you;
he is powerful among you. Although he
was crucified in weakness, he now lives by
the power of God. We, too, are weak, just
as Christ was, but when we deal
with you we will be alive with him and
will have God's power.

2 Corinthians 13:3–4

When You Are Weak

May God replace your painful
memories with redemptive dreams.

May He heal old wounds and pour in timeless wisdom.

May He shore up your weaknesses and shine through your
strengths.

And tonight, may your sleep replenish you in every way.

You are loved and blessed.

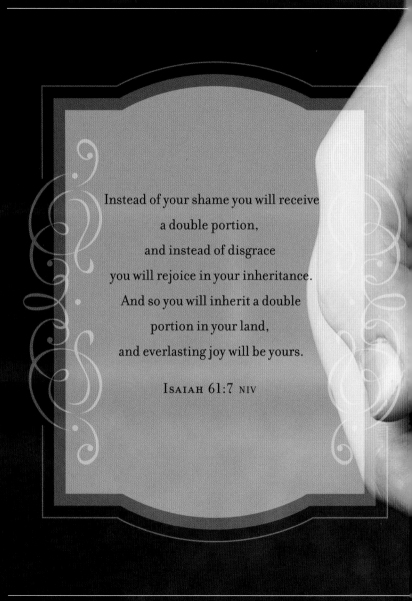

Instead of your shame you will receive

a double portion,

and instead of disgrace

you will rejoice in your inheritance.

And so you will inherit a double

portion in your land,

and everlasting joy will be yours.

Isaiah 61:7 NIV

May the Lord take your frustrations and give you peace; may He carry your burdens and give you grace; may He fill your cup and give you joy.

May peace, grace, and joy mark your life in a beautiful, noticeable way that compels others to look up.

And tonight may He give you divine dreams that nourish your soul and strengthen your faith.

Sleep well. You are blessed.

Take delight in the LORD,

and he will give you

the desires of

your heart.

PSALM 37:4 NIV

Desires of Your Heart

May the Lord fulfill the desires
of your heart and stir up a fresh
passion for His Word.

May He lift a load you're not assigned to carry.

And may He strengthen you to carry your very
important God-assignment.

Sleep well.

And now, dear brothers and sisters, one final thing. Fix your thoughts on what is true, and honorable, and right, and pure, and lovely, and admirable. Think about things that are excellent and worthy of praise. Keep putting into practice all you learned and received from me—everything you heard from me and saw me doing. Then the God of peace will be with you.

PHILIPPIANS

4:8–9

The Right Focus

May the Lord refresh your soul and
renew your perspective.

Though you have reasons to worry,
you have more reasons for faith.

May you put your face in His hands
and fix your eyes on Him.

Ask Him to fill you with blessed assurance
this hour so you'll sleep deeply tonight.

He's got you.

For it is by grace you have been saved,
through faith—and this is not from yourselves, it
is the gift of God—not by works,
so that no one can boast.
For we are God's handiwork, created in
Christ Jesus to do good works,
which God prepared in advance
for us to do.

EPHESIANS 2:8–10 NIV

Created for Good

May you have eyes to see God's best will in every situation; may you have ears to hear His precious voice at every turn.

May you have words that bring hope and healing to every hardship.

And may your steps take you from one divine appointment to another.

Be safe. Sleep well.

You are loved.

For the LORD your God
is living among you.
He is a mighty savior.
He will take delight in you
with gladness.
With his love, he will calm
all your fears.
He will rejoice over you
with joyful songs.

ZEPHANIAH 3:17

Healing Joy

May God unearth the unsettled and unhealed places
in your life so He can heal, renew, and restore you.

May He give you a new revelation of His love
and His grace.

May He give you pools of blessing to splash your feet in.

May His unfathomable greatness bring a fresh mystery
and power to your prayers and perspective.

And tonight, may you sleep deeply and sweetly.

A single day in your courts is better than a thousand anywhere else! I would rather be a gatekeeper in the house of my God than live the good life in the homes of the wicked. For the LORD God is our sun and our shield. He gives us grace and glory. The LORD will withhold no good thing from those who do what is right. O LORD of Heaven's Armies, what joy for those who trust in you.

PSALM 84:10–12

New Heights

May God impart to you
a new level of faith and
expectancy.

May He stir up a new passion for
serving Him.

May He release in you a new level of insight and
grant you a sharper perspective.

May He lead you to new heights with Him so you can believe
Him for great things!

And tonight, may you sleep deeply.

See, I have engraved you

on the palms of my hands;

your walls are ever before me.

ISAIAH 49:16 NIV

In (and From) God's Hands

May you know, on a
deeper level, how much
God loves you.

May you understand in
your heart and mind
how rich you are
because of Him.

May you walk in holy confidence because
you lack no good thing.

And may you remain gracious and humble
because you know that every gift is from Him.

Sleep well.

May God give you more and more grace and peace as you grow in your knowledge of God and Jesus our Lord. By his divine power, God has given us everything we need for living a godly life. We have received all of this by coming to know him, the one who called us to himself by means of his marvelous glory and excellence.

2 Peter 1:2–3

Tenacious Faith

May you walk in Christ's authority, rest in His care,
and live under His divine protection.

May you pray with passion, speak with precision,
and listen with discernment.

May you have the grit and grace to go after everything
God has promised you.

You have all you need to live an other-worldly life.

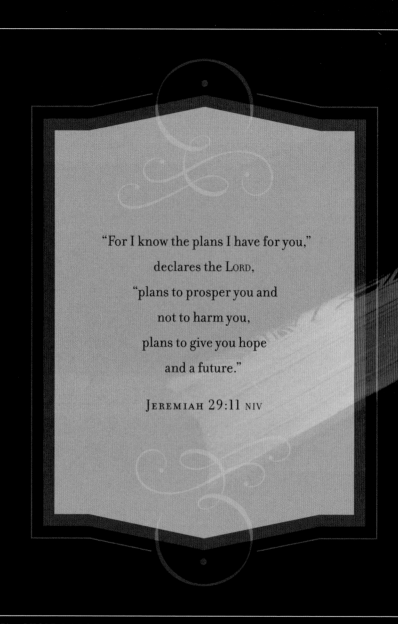

"For I know the plans I have for you,"
declares the LORD,
"plans to prosper you and
not to harm you,
plans to give you hope
and a future."

JEREMIAH 29:11 NIV

Your Divine Purpose

May God himself pour out a fresh anointing on your passions,
a fresh fire on your convictions, and the oil of joy into your soul.

May you take your first steps into tomorrow with deep insight,
focused purposefulness, and Christlike love.

And tonight, may the Lord download fresh revelation about
your life and your divine purpose even while you sleep.

A blessed and beautiful night to you.

Attention, all! See the marvels of GOD!
He plants flowers and trees all over the
earth, bans war from pole to pole,
breaks all the weapons across his knee.
"Step out of the traffic!
Take a long, loving look at me,
your High God, above politics,
above everything."

PSALM 46:8–10 THE MESSAGE

Unhurried Days

May you step out of the hurriedness of the day and step into a pace
that allows for face-to-face conversation with those you love.

May you tighten your belt of truth and let go of the lie that
says you carry your burden alone.

May you set your face like flint and trust God's promise
to carry and establish you.

And may you enjoy deep healing sleep tonight.

Your Redeemer is strong.

Surely the righteous will never be
shaken; they will be remembered
forever. They will have no fear of
bad news; their hearts are steadfast,
trusting in the LORD. Their hearts are
secure, they will have no fear;
in the end they will look in triumph
on their foes.

PSALM 112:6–8 NIV

A Secure Heart

May your capacity for the things of God increase and your understanding of His love exponentially grow.

May your faith in His promises be steadfast and your view of yourself be healed because He loves you.

Sleep well.

Because of the LORD's great love
we are not consumed,
for his compassions never fail.
They are new every morning;
great is your faithfulness.
I say to myself,
"The LORD is my portion;
therefore I will wait for him."

LAMENTATIONS 3:22–24 NIV

Morning Mercies

May you rest tonight knowing that fresh mercies will greet you in the morning, grace will cover you throughout the day, and God's power will be available to you when you need it.

May regret, shame, and insecurity be far removed from you.

May holy confidence and humble dependence mark your life in every way.

Sleep deeply tonight.

Now to him who is able to
do immeasurably more than
all we ask or imagine,
according to his power that is at work
within us, to him be glory in the church
and in Christ Jesus throughout all
generations, for ever and ever!
Amen.

EPHESIANS 3:20–21 NIV

From Impossible to Possible

(Speak this over yourself):

I am deeply loved, divinely appointed,
abundantly equipped, and profoundly
cherished by God.

No enemy plan, scheme, or obstacle can keep me
from God's highest and best will for me.

As I follow the voice of my Savior, I see the invisible,
accomplish the impossible, and love the unlovable.

I am a living, breathing miracle because
Jesus Christ lives in me!

Amen.

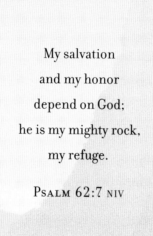

My salvation
and my honor
depend on God;
he is my mighty rock,
my refuge.

Psalm 62:7 NIV

Release Your Burdens

As you end your day, may you release your burdens
and cling more firmly to faith.

May you release your criticisms and choose
to believe the best.

And may you rest in the knowledge that both
your salvation and your honor depend on God alone.

He is your mighty rock and refuge.

Praise be to the God and Father
of our Lord Jesus Christ,
who has blessed us
in the heavenly realms with every
spiritual blessing in Christ.

EPHESIANS 1:3 NIV

An Unlimited Supply

May God grant you a fresh perspective of His unlimited supply.

May you trust Him
with your needs and desires.

May He breathe fresh life into your
soul and fresh power into your dreams.

May you refuse to let your fears and insecurities
speak louder than God's voice.

Even as you sleep, may your ears be fine-tuned to heaven's song
over you, for it is redemptive, beautiful, and life-giving!

Rest well.

Blessings for Specific Needs
and Occasions

There remains, then, a Sabbath-rest

for the people of God;

for anyone who enters God's rest

also rests from their works,

just as God did from his.

Let us, therefore, make every effort

to enter that rest,

so that no one will perish

by following their example

of disobedience.

Hebrews 4:9–11 NIV

Sabbath Rest

For the next twenty-four hours, may God help you engage in true Sabbath rest.

May you unhitch from the daily burden, the daily yoke, and the daily concerns that are yours.

May you pause long enough to pray, be present enough to enjoy another's company, and slow down
enough to rest.

And above all, may you worship
the One who gave you the Sabbath.

Sleep well!

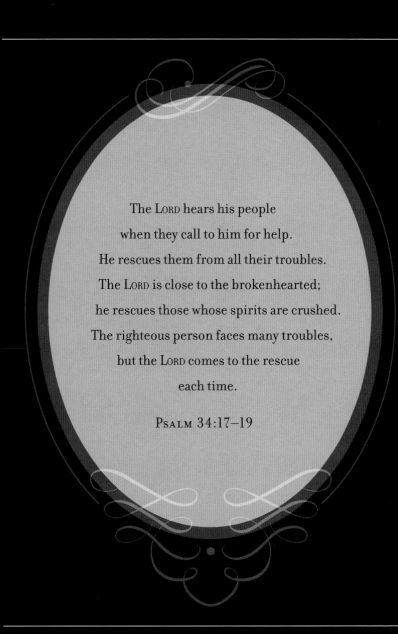

The Lord hears his people
when they call to him for help.
He rescues them from all their troubles.
The Lord is close to the brokenhearted;
he rescues those whose spirits are crushed.
The righteous person faces many troubles,
but the Lord comes to the rescue
each time.

Psalm 34:17–19

Grief

May God himself surround you with tender mercies
and divine strength.

May He heal your broken heart and restore your sense of hope.

May He give you precious times of rest while you work
through your grief.

And may He show you that He's not finished with you yet.

He has a beautiful plan that will bless your heart.

He'll restore and redeem every lost thing!

Rest in Him today.

Bless you.

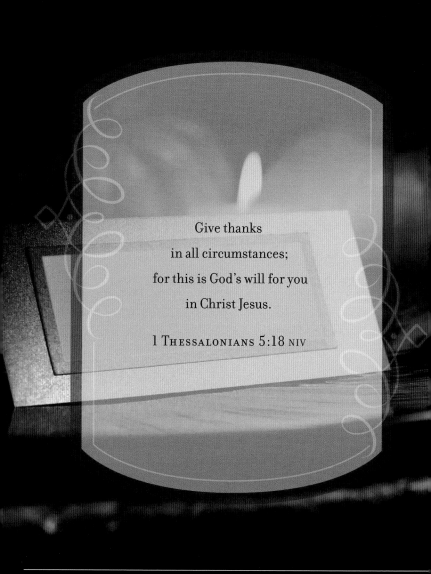

Give thanks
in all circumstances;
for this is God's will for you
in Christ Jesus.

1 Thessalonians 5:18 NIV

Thanksgiving Day

On this eve of Thanksgiving Day, may you set aside your fears, worries, and frustrations, and pull close the ones you love.

May you savor every bite of nourishment God provides.

May you notice sacred moments and give thanks for all that is right in your world.

May the Lord make himself especially real to you in the coming days.

And may you grow in your capacity to thank Him and trust Him.

Enjoy your holiday.

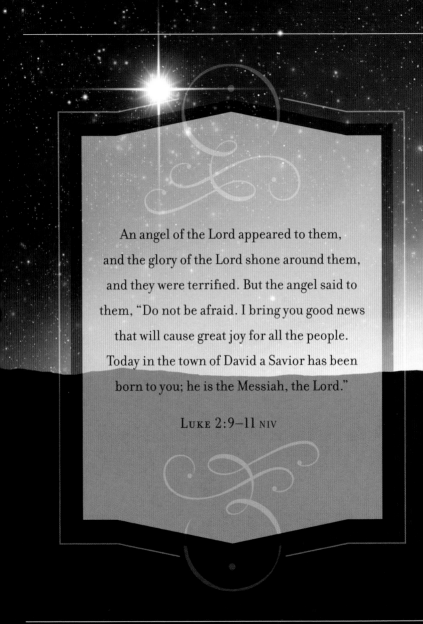

An angel of the Lord appeared to them,
and the glory of the Lord shone around them,
and they were terrified. But the angel said to
them, "Do not be afraid. I bring you good news
that will cause great joy for all the people.
Today in the town of David a Savior has been
born to you; he is the Messiah, the Lord."

LUKE 2:9–11 NIV

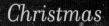

Christmas

May the reality that Christ came to earth for you stir in you
a fresh sense of wonder and awe.

May the power of His love pour in and spill out of you.

May the treasure of His nearness give you safe assurance
that you're never alone.

And may the price He paid to save you remind you
that He will always be there for you.

Sweet and peaceful dreams to you!

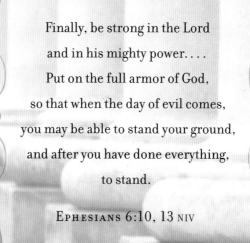

Finally, be strong in the Lord
and in his mighty power. . . .
Put on the full armor of God,
so that when the day of evil comes,
you may be able to stand your ground,
and after you have done everything,
to stand.

EPHESIANS 6:10, 13 NIV

Spiritual Warfare

May God prove himself strong on your behalf.

May He show you how to wisely and strategically stand in this place.

May you raise your shield of faith and block every fiery arrow the enemy sends your way.

May you point your sword and dismantle every enemy scheme fashioned against you.

May you know God's loving and intimate presence right here, right now.

And may you experience firsthand how mighty, how powerful, and how faithful He truly is.

God is mighty to save, He's with you in battle, and He's equipped you to win.

May blessed and nourishing sleep be yours tonight!

Yes, I am the vine; you are the branches. Those who remain in me, and I in them, will produce much fruit. For apart from me you can do nothing. Anyone who does not remain in me is thrown away like a useless branch and withers. Such branches are gathered into a pile to be burned. But if you remain in me and my words remain in you, you may ask for anything you want, and it will be granted! When you produce much fruit, you are my true disciples. This brings great glory to my Father.

JOHN 15:5–8

Disappointment

May God take all of your failures, hardships, and heartbreaks, and carry them for you.

May you suddenly feel light in step and spirit.

May you trust that brighter days are ahead, and may you look up expectantly as you wait for God to keep His word to you.

Rest well.

Acknowledgments

Special thanks to:

*My friends at Bethany House Publishers—
for seeing the beauty in these blessings*

My literary agent, Steve Laube—for giving my message wings

My assistant, Lisa Irwin—for serving in the most excellent way

My intercessors—for your consistent, faithful, powerful prayers

My friends and family—for your love and presence in my life

My Savior, Jesus—for all that You are to me

SUSIE LARSON is a popular radio host, national speaker, and author. She cohosts the Focus on the Family radio show *Everyday Relationships with Dr. Greg Smalley* and also has her own talk show, *Live the Promise with Susie Larson*. Her passion is to see men and women everywhere strengthened in their faith and mobilized to live out their high calling in Jesus Christ.

Her seven previous books include *Your Beautiful Purpose*, *Growing Grateful Kids*, *The Uncommon Woman*, and *Embracing Your Freedom*.

Susie and her husband, Kevin, live near Minneapolis, Minnesota, and have three adult sons. For more information, visit www.susie larson.com.

May the Lord bless you
and protect you.

May the Lord smile on you
and be gracious to you.

May the Lord show you his favor
and give you his peace.

—Numbers 6:24–26